A GUIDE ON A.I. ART

& HOW TO MAKE MONEY

RAYA WIN

TABLE OF CONTENTS

INTRODUCTION

Maximizing Your AI Art Potential: A Comprehensive Guide

Over the past few years, AI art has surged in popularity. There's a growing interest in creating AI art and a thriving market of eager buyers willing to pay top dollar for the right piece. Unfortunately, many beginners make costly mistakes and struggle to sell their work.

But fear not! This guide is designed to equip you with the techniques you need to create stunning AI art that resonates with the market and fetches a high price. Regardless of your artistic background or experience, our step-by-step guide will take you through everything you need to know to succeed with AI art.

We've put in the hard work to provide you with a comprehensive resource that covers all aspects of creating and selling AI art. You'll learn proven techniques to create the highest-quality AI art that the market demands, as well as strategies to sell it for a good profit. So, let's get started on your profitable journey into the exciting world of AI art!

CHAPTER 1

What is AI Art?

Artificial Intelligence (AI) has evolved from being a niche interest to a technology that we use in almost every aspect of our daily lives. AI is evident in self-driving cars, digital assistants such as Siri, Google Assistant, and Alexa, virtual personal assistants on our computers, smartphones, and other devices, as well as smart home appliances. AI's influence on our lives is growing more prominent every day.

Apart from these visible applications, there are still more undiscovered uses of AI. One of these emerging fields is Artificial Intelligence Art (AI Art) - the practice of using AI techniques to create art. Although computer scientists have been using AI to generate images since the 1980s, it has only recently become a new medium for artistic expression.

Using Mathematical Algorithms to Generate Art

Artificial Intelligence (AI) is a computer science subset that enables machines to behave like humans. It involves creating machines that can comprehend the world around them, grasp concepts, and make decisions based on this information.

The Power of AI in Art: Understanding its Role in Creativity

AI has the ability to perform tasks that would be challenging or even impossible for humans, such as diagnosing illnesses or detecting patterns in vast amounts of data. AI art, a branch of AI, involves using computers to create works of art. Artists who create art using AI are known as AI artists.

Artists have been generating and manipulating images with computers since the 1950s, using software code, mathematical algorithms, and computer graphics models. However, this form of computer art is not considered AI art, as it does not involve machine learning or other types of artificial intelligence.

Generating Art through Computer Instructions: A Collaboration between Artists and AI

The creative process behind AI art is similar to how traditional artists approach their work. The artist begins by conceptualizing an idea for a piece, whether it's a landscape, portrait, or something abstract. One method of creating AI art involves starting with a sketch. This serves as a blueprint, enabling the artist to plan their creative process and execute the final work in a way that best expresses their artistic intent.

Next, the artist composes the artwork by providing instructions to the computer on how to manipulate mathematical algorithms and computer-generated images to achieve the desired aesthetic and artistic effect. Essentially, the artist creates a set of rules and guidelines that the computer follows to generate a final piece of art.

Thanks to platforms like Midjourney, non-artists can now create AI art by providing text instructions and "keywords." We'll delve into this further in our guide.

The Versatility of AI Art for Artists and Non-Artists Alike
Art is a process that requires trial and error, with many artists going back to their work until they perfect it. Computers, on the other hand, are incredibly efficient and consistent in their execution of tasks, thus AI can help artists work more effectively and consistently, giving them more time to perfect their craft and experiment with new ideas.

Furthermore, computers can utilize a vast amount of data and existing information to generate new types of art. Sometimes, AI is programmed to create entirely fresh and surprising outcomes.

AI-generated art provides artistic creators with the opportunity to explore new concepts, create something distinct from their previous works, and even challenge their preconceived notions about artistic expression. And this technology is also available to non-artists, allowing them to bring to life the images they have in their minds.

AI Art: A New Medium for Creative Expression
Artists have been dabbling with AI since the 1980s, but only recently has technology become a platform for artistic expression. As computer scientists continue to refine their programming, AI is becoming increasingly sophisticated and advanced, resulting in more intricate and high-quality work.

These advancements have opened new doors for artists interested in experimenting with AI, and have also captured the attention of scholars, media outlets, and the public. AI art has emerged as a distinct genre, and more people are exploring the technology's artistic potential.

Exploring the Unique Aesthetic of AI Art

AI technology is transforming the way we approach art, with the public and AI artists alike contributing to its vast development. From visual art pieces to music and poetry, the possibilities are endless. The creative vision of the artist and the technology used to generate the artwork determine the final product's appearance.

The tools that AI artists use, such as programming languages, computer graphics models, and algorithms, can vary significantly, resulting in a wide range of styles and aesthetics. While some artists rely on machine learning techniques to produce their designs, most use programming languages and algorithms to create their art.

Creating AI Art is Easier Than You Think

Artists have been utilizing computers to create art since the 1950s, and since the 1980s, they have been using AI to create even more complex pieces. With technology advancements, AI has become an essential tool for artists to generate new designs, improve workflows, and explore new creative concepts. It's also an excellent opportunity for artists who want to experiment with AI as an artistic medium. This guide will show you how to create stunning AI art that you can sell.

Advancements in AI Art Technology Persist

The mesmerizing world of AI art is on a wild ride, and nobody knows where it will end up! One thing's for sure, it's only going to get better with age. As artists continue to tinker with AI, they'll unleash a whole new universe of inspiring and mind-bending creations.

The philosophical implications of AI art are currently being debated by artists. They're pondering questions such as, "What does it mean for a computer to create art?" and "How do we define what art is?" AI art offers a unique perspective on humanity as a whole, and artists are eager to explore it further.

If you're not interested in these philosophical questions, don't worry. This guide is here to help you create AI art easily and sell it for profit – regardless of whether you have any artistic skills. This is a new and exciting market, so you'll be joining at the perfect time.

In the following chapter, we'll delve into the many benefits of creating AI art.

CHAPTER 2

The Benefits of Creating AI Art

Artificial Intelligence (AI) has seeped into every industry, including art. However, this doesn't mean that AI can create masterpieces like Picasso or Van Gogh. Instead, it helps artists and individuals produce their work faster and with greater precision than before. With the aid of AI algorithms and effective tools, anyone can unleash their creative potential and create art that was once impossible to produce.

Here are some benefits of using AI in art:

- No artistic talent is needed to create AI art. Even if you have no artistic ability, AI algorithms that are pre-trained can assist you in creating art by inputting the relevant style, content, and desired outcome.
- Algorithms that are pre-trained can produce art that is similar in style to that of major artists. You can post-process your AI-generated art to make it appear more realistic.
- With AI art platforms currently available, even beginners can effortlessly create high-quality images. Understanding how the platform works and providing accurate instructions is all that is required.
- As technology advances, creating stunning AI art will become even easier, making it possible for everyone to produce beautiful artwork regardless of their level of artistic talent.

Using AI to Spark Your Creativity

If you're struggling to find inspiration, consider using AI as a tool to assist you. By employing a neural network, you can discover images that are similar to pieces of art that you admire, serving as a starting point for your own artistic endeavors.

Once you've gathered a collection of inspirational images, you can curate them into a mood board or collage, which can be referred back to when you're feeling stuck or lacking in confidence.

AI can serve as a source of inspiration for artists of all skill levels, so don't be discouraged if you're not an experienced artist. With technology at your fingertips, creativity can flourish in anyone.

Creating Art Instantly using AI

Artificial intelligence is a great tool for producing art efficiently. In need of a quick piece of art? AI can help.

Generative adversarial networks (GANs) are algorithms that use labeled data to create images based on a specific style. By training GANs, you can produce images quickly, though some post-production may be necessary to finalize your work.

This technology is particularly useful for fast sketches or visual notes, such as doodles. GANs are also a great option for artists who require quick sketches for upcoming exhibitions.

Platforms like Midjourney provide an easy-to-use AI art platform for anyone to create impressive images quickly. Simply provide text instructions and the AI will generate images based on your specifications.

Using AI to Simplify Color Selection

Creating the perfect color palette for your artwork can be a challenging task, but AI art platforms can make it a breeze. These systems can scan images to identify dominant colors and generate a palette that you can use to create similar-looking artworks with ease.

This feature is particularly useful for establishing a consistent brand, whether you're designing logos, branding, or posters. Additionally, it can help you set the tone or mood you're aiming for in your artwork by selecting the most fitting colors. Trust AI to help you pick the perfect colors for your art.

Facial Recognition Made Easy with AI

Artificial Intelligence can make face detection and tracking easier for you if you're working on an image or portrait that includes a person. You can use a pre-trained model and open-source machine learning libraries to identify and track faces. This feature is especially useful for portrait artists who want to ensure that their work is as precise as possible.

Automating Repetitive Tasks with AI

AI is a powerful tool that can be used to automate repetitive tasks, saving you valuable time and effort. This is particularly useful for artists who are creating a lot of work, such as a series of paintings, prints, or branding images.

By utilizing algorithms, you can easily automate tasks like color selection, image resizing, and file naming, streamlining your workflow and allowing you to create art more efficiently. This can help you produce more work in less time, giving you the freedom to focus on the creative process.

Selling Your AI Art: A Promising Opportunity

If you're proud of your AI art creations, you can sell them for a higher price than traditional art. Set it at a price you're comfortable with and market it on various platforms such as AI Art, Artsy, social media, or galleries.

With the growing demand for AI art, you can turn this into a profitable career by producing enough pieces and using the right marketing strategy. By venturing into AI art, you get a chance to stand out from the crowd.

In the next chapter, we'll share the best strategies for selling your AI art at a premium price and how to prepare for creating stunning pieces that sell. Don't miss this chance to be a part of the increasing demand for AI art.

CHAPTER 3

Prepare to Create Stunning AI Art that will Sell

From Text to Stunning Visuals

Creators of AI art may use different tools and techniques, but they all share a common goal: to convert plain text into visually stunning, thought-provoking and beautiful images. By leveraging algorithms and software, artists can turn words into pictures that captivate the viewer's imagination.

While AI-generated art may not be everyone's cup of tea, it's growing in popularity. Digital paintings of iconic fictional characters like Harry Potter, the Teenage Mutant Ninja Turtles, and Sherlock Holmes, along with digitally distorted photographs that appear almost unrecognizable as real people, are just a few examples of the diverse range of AI art that often challenges the viewer's senses.

In this chapter, we will guide you through the essential steps required to create remarkable AI art from text prompts. Being prepared is crucial, as many people dive into AI art platforms without the right knowledge and fail to create art that can be sold.

Understanding Your Audience: Creating AI Art for Profit and Social Media

If you're considering creating AI art to make money or grow your social media following, it's important to know your audience. Who would be interested in viewing your work? Are you aiming for a specific niche? While AI art is a unique way to create art from text prompts, it may not be suitable for everyone.

Some people may find it intriguing, while others may find it difficult to comprehend or uninteresting. However, if you're creating AI art for your own pleasure, that's perfectly fine too. The beauty of creativity is that it can lead to unexpected discoveries and useful applications.

Maximizing Your AI Art Sales by Understanding Your Audience To increase your success in selling AI art, having a clear understanding of your audience's preferences is crucial. Take the time to research what is currently popular and who is buying it. In no time, you'll become familiar with the market and be able to capitalize on it to generate the highest earnings.

Exploring AI Art: Research and Inspiration

When it comes to creating AI artwork, there are plenty of paths you can take. As you begin researching, keep an open mind and explore different types of AI art. It's important to understand how the algorithms and processes work behind each type so you can create something that's both visually appealing and meaningful for your audience.

How to Collect Inspiration for AI Artwork

To create unique AI artwork, it's important to gather inspiration from various sources. Don't limit yourself to just one type of AI art. Explore different algorithms that generate digital paintings, photos, distorted images, or text-based art.

Consider exploring different styles of AI artwork, such as minimalism, realism, or surrealism, to gain inspiration for various approaches to AI artwork. It's essential to know your audience's preferences, so be prepared to conduct thorough research to deliver the best results.

Exploring Layouts and Shapes for Your AI Artwork

Choosing how to present your AI artwork is crucial, and there are many options to consider. You can opt for a line layout, shape layout, or a hybrid of both. Depending on your layout preference, you may also want to experiment with different shapes.

For example, if you're designing a digital painting, a line layout can help you create a visually clean and consistent artwork.

When working with shapes, consider trying out various shapes, such as squares, circles, triangles, hexagons, or even polygons, to elevate your design. You can even use triangles and hexagons to construct a grid layout.

Choosing the Right Type of AI Art to Create

Now that you've explored the various types of AI artwork, it's time to decide which one you'd like to create. Keep in mind that not all algorithms are suitable for every type of AI art.

For instance, your algorithm may only support text-based art, but you may want to create a digital painting. Therefore, it's important to check the capabilities of the platform you plan to use. In our guide, we will explore the best AI art platforms.

Although you can create any type of AI art you desire, some are more popular than others, such as distorted images, digital paintings, and text-based art. If you're a digital painter, creating portraits of fictional characters is a popular choice. You can depict famous characters from books, movies, TV shows, or even video games.

Get to Know Your AI Art Platform for Optimal Results

Whether or not you're planning on creating AI art, it's crucial to be familiar with the software and tools at your disposal. Your fluency with the AI art platform will influence the quality of your work and your overall productivity. If you're considering monetizing your art, it's also important to have a grasp of tools like Midjourney, which can help you create visually stunning pieces in a snap.

It's worth noting that some AI art platforms may require algorithm training. The more data you provide, the better the algorithm's performance will be. To ensure the software you're considering is appropriate for your needs, read reviews and learn about other creators' experiences. This includes assessing the ease of use and the kind of results you can expect from the software.

Understanding the Process behind AI-generated Art

Before delving into the world of AI art, it's crucial to comprehend how it's created. Artificial intelligence artists rely on algorithms to translate words into images. These algorithms analyze each letter of a text, such as a sentence or paragraph, to determine the type of image it should produce.

During the process of creating AI art, the algorithm may generate something different from the initial idea. Since each algorithm has its own set of rules, different artists may produce varying outputs.

For instance, if the word "ninja" is included in the text, one algorithm may generate a ninja-themed image, while another algorithm may generate a Samurai-themed image. These are just a few examples of how algorithms may interpret a word like "ninja" in a text.

Selecting the Visual Style for Your AI Art

Before diving into the creation of AI artwork, take time to decide on a visual style. Although each algorithm has its own set of rules, it's beneficial to have a particular style in mind. For instance, if you plan on creating digital paintings, you may want to consider a surrealistic style. It's worth noting that various types of AI artwork are better suited for some algorithms than others.

For example, distorted image algorithms often pair best with a surrealistic style. So, take some time to explore different types of AI artwork to find what works best for you.

Achieving Optimal Results Through Text Selection in AI Art

To produce the best AI art, it is essential to select the right text. Before creating your piece, review the text you plan to use and ensure it is the best representation of your intended creation. The quality of the text is also crucial. Text that is too long or too short may result in an image that is too long or too short.

It's important to note that the algorithm may struggle to create an image from text that is written in a different language, or if the image quality is poor. For this reason, entering high-quality text into the platform is essential for creating stunning AI art.

Consider the following factors when selecting text for your project:
- Purpose- is it for commercial or personal use?
- Text length - how many words or characters does it contain?
- Language - is the text in English? Keep in mind that AI translates text into images in the language of the machine. To create your AI art piece in English, you need to provide text written in English.
- Image quality - what is the image resolution of the text?

Here are a few types of text that can produce stunning AI art results:
- Poetry - AI art based on poetry can be inspiring, as it is often short and succinct.
- Fiction - if you want to create an AI art piece based on a novel, short story, or series of short stories, you need to make sure that the text is concise.
- Drabble - short pieces of writing are ideal for AI art. Drabble is a type of short story that's written to fit within a certain word count.
- Quotes - quotes are short and often to the point, making them ideal for creating AI art.

Creating the Best AI Art with the Right Commands

To produce an image from the text, it's crucial to provide the AI with the right command. Here are a few ways to achieve this:

- Upload an image to the AI algorithm to find text in the image
- Convert text into an image
- Feed the text into the AI algorithm
- Choose an image and use a keyword search to detect text in the image

By using an image-to-text conversion algorithm, you can apply the same algorithm for both the short and long versions of your AI art piece, with only the colors and fonts varying.

Keep in mind that entering the proper commands into your preferred AI art platform takes practice to produce the desired results. Don't be discouraged if your first attempts don't work out. Keep practicing until you achieve mastery.

In the next chapter, we'll explore the best AI art platforms to create your artwork.

CHAPTER 4

The Best AI Art Platforms to Create your Art

The Impact of Artificial Intelligence on All Industries, Including Art Artificial intelligence has revolutionized the world and has left its mark on every industry. With AI, data can be analyzed more quickly and accurately than ever before. From natural language processing to computer vision, new AI innovations are constantly being developed.

This technological advancement has also influenced the art world, where artists and non-artists alike are using AI to create art pieces that surpass anything that can be created by hand. Although some of the AI art platforms available require payment, they are all relatively inexpensive.

Additionally, one free platform will be discussed in this chapter. Considering the potential to sell high-quality AI art for a good price, the cost of using these platforms is worth it. Let's take a closer look at each of these platforms and what they offer.

Selecting the Right AI Art Platform for Your Needs

Before diving into the world of AI art, it's important to choose an AI platform that suits your preferences. While many platforms allow you to create AI art, some are more user-friendly than others. Consider what features are important to you and what kind of artwork you'd like to create.

Some AI platforms offer a variety of features, while others allow you to create unique artwork. You have many options to choose from when it comes to AI platforms that can help you create your own AI art.

Certain platforms enable you to create art by inputting text, while others require image uploads from which the AI art is generated. There are also platforms that accept both text and image uploads.

In this guide, we'll be discussing the Midjourney platform quite a bit. We believe it to be one of the best platforms available, and it's now easy to sign up for without needing an invitation. However, there are other great platforms out there as well.

The AI Art Platform that Stands Out

Midjourney's AI art is exceptional, and it's one of the reasons we love it. You can now sign up as a beta user and create your AI art on the platform. In the next chapter, we will discuss how to create AI art using Midjourney.

Midjourney isn't just any AI art platform; it's the only one where a user has won a serious art competition with an AI-generated piece. Midjourney's art pieces have a lot of detail that other platforms cannot produce. Once you've mastered it, you can create AI art that rivals human-made art.

Midjourney's unique platform allows you to create your own AI-generated art by entering text commands. You can test it for usability and quality with the free trial version. The platform has a wide variety of features, including creating a range of styles and generating new images based on input text or uploaded images.

Midjourney also has its online community where you can share your AI art and browse others'. It's easy to use and produces AI art quickly.

A Top-Tier AI Art Platform for Your Creative Needs

Jasper Art is a top-tier AI art platform that allows users to create stunning artwork by simply entering text. Unlike many other platforms, Jasper Art is continuously evolving and advancing its technology to offer the best possible experience to users. With Jasper Art, you can explore different art styles and experiment with various commands to create the perfect image.

While Jasper Art may not be as user-friendly as some other platforms, such as Midjourney, it offers a wider range of features and capabilities. To ensure the best results, you must craft your text instructions carefully. However, if you use the right commands, Jasper Art can generate high-quality images quickly and easily, including photo-quality and cartoon images.

Although there is no free trial available at the time of writing, Jasper Art offers affordable pricing starting at $20 per month. The platform also offers support in multiple languages, and their team is always ready to assist you in entering the right commands to create the images you want. Additionally, Jasper Art provides copywriting templates to help you create your art seamlessly. Experience the power of Jasper Art today and take your artistic creations to the next level!

Creating AI Art with Stable Diffusion

Stable Diffusion is a great option if you're interested in generating AI art from pre-existing images. This new AI art platform is from the same developers as NightCafe, which we will also discuss later in this section.

What sets Stable Diffusion apart from other AI art platforms is its ability to create unique AI art using text prompts, in addition to images. Not to mention, it's completely free to use!

Despite being a free platform, the image quality of the art generated by Stable Diffusion is remarkably high. You can easily access Stable Diffusion through a web browser and begin generating AI art images in no time. You're free to use the art you create for commercial or non-commercial purposes without any cost.

One thing to note is that the demo version of Stable Diffusion may take some time to generate art. Depending on the number of jobs in line, it can take between 1 and 15 minutes. We found that generating art from existing images took significantly longer than generating art from text prompts. However, considering that Stable Diffusion is a free platform, this is a minor issue. As long as you use the correct text instructions, the quality of the images created by Stable Diffusion is top-notch and you won't be disappointed with the results.

NightCafe: The Top AI Art Platform for Beginners

NightCafe is one of the most popular AI art platforms available with a plethora of art generation and special algorithms that few other platforms can match. Even if you are new to the world of AI art, NightCafe is a breeze to use, with a free trial that does not require any credit card details.

NightCafe's simple approach lets you generate art by entering your text instructions and letting your imagination soar. The platform is also speedy, usually taking no more than 30 seconds to generate your creations.

Like most platforms, NightCafe produces unique AI art that is sure to delight you. If you enjoy the platform, NightCafe has a credit system where you can pay for credits or earn more by participating in the community. During our testing, we were able to produce high-quality images with minimal effort.

One unique feature of NightCafe is their video generation tools, which are not offered by many other platforms. With NightCafe, you can secure ownership of the art you create. Their community is helpful and supportive.

Pricing plans for NightCafe start at $9.99 for 100 credits, with larger plans available for up to 1500 credits per month.

Photosonic: An AI Image Creation Tool
Photosonic is an innovative AI-powered image creation tool brought to you by the creators of Writesonic, a renowned AI copywriting platform. If you're a content creator looking for related visuals, Photosonic is the perfect solution for you.

With Photosonic, you can either input your own text to generate unique artwork or choose from a range of pre-existing images and customize them to your liking. With support for various art styles, you have plenty of options to choose from. Creating photo images or cartoon-style artwork is a breeze with Photosonic.

One of the most impressive features of Photosonic is its ability to convert your images into paintings. Try out the free trial and witness the outstanding results for yourself. The free version provides two art outputs after entering your text prompt.

Photosonic also offers the option to enlarge your images for added enhancement. The pricing for credits is very reasonable. The Basic plan provides 100 credits for just $10 per month, while the unlimited credit plan is available for $25 a month.

DALL-E 2: The Ultimate AI Art Creation Platform

Initially available only via invitation, DALL-E 2 now offers a beta sign-up for users. Developed by OpenAI, the platform is renowned for producing some of the most impressive photorealistic images in the industry. But that's not all - DALL-E 2 is versatile enough to create illustrations, business ideas, and product design prototypes. Our team tested the AI art capabilities of the program and was thoroughly impressed.

One of the most useful features of DALL-E 2 is its paintbrush tool. You can easily modify an image by highlighting the area you want to change and entering text instructions. The paintbrush tool will then implement the changes for you.

To create AI art, simply enter text instructions or use the image-to-image editor. You can also upload an existing image and specify the changes you want to make. DALL-E 2 allows for multiple iterations of your AI art, making the possibilities endless.

While a free trial is available, the program requires credits for continued use. The pricing structure is not entirely clear, but you can purchase 115 credits for $15, which is enough to create over 450 images sized at 1024 by 1024 pixels.

CHAPTER 5

Getting Started with Midjourney

If you're not a software engineer and don't have an AI developer at your disposal, creating an AI-powered digital art project may seem like a daunting challenge. Fortunately, Midjourney.com is here to help. This up-and-coming website is tailored for individuals with limited technical knowledge and artistic ability, allowing for the creation of AI-powered art projects through special text prompts.

Follow this chapter to learn how to use Midjourney.com and create your own AI-powered artwork in no time!

Your One-Stop Destination for AI-Powered Artwork

Midjourney.com offers an easy way to create AI-powered art. With this website, you can create a variety of artwork without the need for any artistic talent or engineering knowledge. Examples include digital paintings, 3D scenes, and digital drawings of faces.

Midjourney's AI technology works with simple text prompts, allowing you to create stunning artwork in seconds. You can also transform existing images using the platform. So why wait? Start creating your own AI-powered art with Midjourney today.

Experience Midjourney's Beta Version Today!

Sign up as a beta user at Midjourney.com and gain immediate and limitless access to the platform. Joining as a beta user is easier than ever before, as you no longer have to wait for an invitation to join. You can explore Midjourney's AI art creation capabilities for free and without delay.

As a beta user, you're able to create up to 25 AI art pieces each month at no cost. However, to generate additional AI art images, you'll need to purchase credits using their credit system. The pricing plan is reasonable, and you can earn a good return on investment by selling your AI art creations. More details on this will be provided in a later chapter. Best of all, there's no need to download any software or install any programs with Midjourney.

How to Access Midjourney via Discord

Midjourney is an entirely anonymous platform, which means that to use it, you'll need to access it through Discord. Discord is a free online chat app that allows you to create virtual chat rooms that can be accessed via a web browser, computer, or mobile app. If you don't already have a Discord account, you can create one for free at discord.gg.

To get started with Midjourney, simply sign up as a Beta User, and you'll receive a link that will take you directly to the Midjourney conversation room on Discord. From there, you can begin exploring the platform's features and even create your own AI art.

Begin in a Newcomer Room

To fully experience Midjourney, we suggest starting with a visit to a Newcomer Midjourney conversation room on Discord. Here, as a newcomer, you can delve into the features of Midjourney and create multiple AI art samples. Most Midjourney conversation rooms welcome newcomers with open arms.

Access a Newcomer conversation room for Midjourney by clicking on the link provided when you sign up as a Beta User.

Creating AI Art with Text Prompts

Midjourney is an exciting platform that allows you to produce AI art by using text prompts. As a Beta User, you can access the platform via Discord and begin exploring the features. A text prompt is simply a brief phrase that outlines the type of art you want to generate with Midjourney. There are several pre-loaded text prompts available that you can use to produce AI art samples. However, the best way to start is by creating a custom text prompt of your own. With a text prompt that you've created, Midjourney enables you to generate a wide range of unique art pieces.

Enhance Your AI Art with the Upscaling Feature

Midjourney allows you to elevate your AI-generated artwork with its upscaling feature. Not only can you transform your sample into a full-fledged piece of digital art, but you can also create a 3D model with ease.

Utilize the "U" buttons (U1, U2, U3, U4) to execute the upscaling process on the four images that Midjourney generates. Once you're satisfied with the outcome, you can share your artwork online or download it as a file to create a unique digital art installation that incorporates AI technology.

Generating AI Art Variations

Did you know that you can create multiple variations of your AI artwork with Midjourney? Once you've designed your initial piece, simply use the "V" buttons (V1, V2, V3 and V4) to produce up to four different versions of your creation. Moreover, you can utilize a text prompt to modify your artwork and make it stand out.

Mastering Midjourney: Tips for Creating Incredible AI Art

Midjourney is packed with powerful features that can help you create stunning AI art. However, don't expect to become a pro overnight. There is a learning curve, but it's not insurmountable.

Take advantage of the Midjourney Discord groups to learn from others and practice using the platform's various features. By examining the commands used by other users to create their AI art, you can gain valuable insights and achieve the results you desire.

In the following chapter, we will delve into the best Midjourney text prompts to use for creating exceptional AI art.

CHAPTER 6

Use the Best Text Prompts for Excellent AI Art Results

In this chapter, we will concentrate on the prompts that are specific to Midjourney. However, this principle can be applied to any AI art platform that you use. Employing the most suitable text prompts is crucial to achieving the best results with your AI-generated art. It's beneficial to explore various text prompts, allowing you to produce the AI art that best suits your needs.

Getting Started with AI Art on Midjourney

Are you ready to dive into the world of AI art with Midjourney? It all starts with the command /imagine, followed by a space and your prompt. Head over to the Midjourney newcomer channel on Discord where you'll find a text box at the bottom. Once you've entered your prompt in the following format: /imagine prompt description, hit "enter".

The Midjourney AI algorithms will then begin creating your AI art. Keep in mind that with thousands of users entering prompts simultaneously, it may take some time for your art to appear. You can track the progress of your image as it uploads in percentage format.

Getting the Best AI Art Results

It's important to keep in mind that the first prompt you enter may not yield the results you're hoping for. Don't worry – perfecting your AI art with Midjourney will take time and practice. In the Newcomer rooms, you can see examples of AI art that didn't turn out well due to the prompts entered by the users.

When Midjourney creates your AI art, it will display four different variations in a 2x2 grid. Below the image grid, you'll find buttons that allow you to upscale your images (using the U buttons to make your images bigger) or make variations to your images using the V buttons.

Enhancing Your Prompts with Multiple Adjectives

It's common for new users to enter prompts with only one adjective and be surprised when the result doesn't meet their expectations. To create a vivid image, it's essential to use more than one adjective. For instance, if you want to generate an image of a bird, "a colorful bird" may not produce the desired outcome. Instead, try adding more adjectives, such as "a multi-colored bird flying at sunset across a field of beautiful flowers." With this approach, you can use two adjectives, "multi-colored" and "beautiful," to create a more captivating image.

Provide Specific Prompts

The more detailed your prompts are, the better results you can expect from the AI art generated by Midjourney. By giving the AI more options to work with, you'll see a significant improvement in the quality of the final product. It's always a good idea to have a clear image in your mind of what you want the AI to create for you.

To achieve the best outcome, try to articulate your vision as accurately as possible. For instance, if you want an image of a bird soaring over a field of vibrant flowers during sunset, describe it in detail. This will give Midjourney a lot of information to work with and produce better images that align with your vision.

Improve Your Results with Familiar Words

To enhance your prompts, try incorporating well-known words and phrases. For instance:

- King
- Queen
- Knight
- Dragon
- Wizard

Since Midjourney has millions of image references in its databases, using familiar terms helps connect your prompt with the right set of images. There are likely to be many references with the "king" label, for example. By using common words and phrases, you can create better AI art.

Including Your Desired Artistic Style in Your Prompt

If you want your AI art to reflect a specific artistic style, it's essential to include this in your prompt so that Midjourney can deliver the desired result. Remember, we are dealing with machines, not human minds, so providing clear instructions is crucial.

Here are a few examples of artistic styles that you could incorporate into your prompts:

- Abstract
- Contemporary
- Cubism
- Cyberpunk
- Fantasy
- Impressionism
- Minimal
- Modern
- Surrealism

By giving Midjourney this useful information, you can help it create the type of AI art you're looking for. It may take some time to become familiar with the right prompts, but the more imaginative you are, the better your AI art will turn out.

Improving Your AI Art with Common Midjourney Prompts
If you want to create the best AI art, it's important to have a diverse prompt vocabulary. While this list isn't comprehensive, it's a great starting point to enhance your art using common midjourney prompts. Take a look at these frequently used prompts:

- Dynamic
- Atmospheric
- Futurism
- Dramatic lighting
- Maximum texture
- Anthropomorphic
- Time loop
- 8k

- Concept art
- Very detailed
- Multiverse
- Cinematic lighting
- Atompunk
- Unreal engine
- Symmetrical
- Octane render
- Ray tracing
- Photorealistic
- Bionic futurism
- Hyperrealistic
- Steampunk
- Sharp focus
- Cyberpunk
- Rim lighting
- Iridescent
- Soft lighting
- Internal glow
- Volumetric
- Studio light
- Surreal
- HDR
- Fantastic backlight
- Realistic CGI

By using these prompts, you can describe what you want your AI art to look like in terms that the computers can understand. Remember, this isn't a definitive list, and you can add your own prompts to personalize your art.

Entering Your Prompts Correctly: Commas and Spaces Are Key

When inputting prompts into Midjourney, it's crucial to follow the correct format in order to achieve the desired results. Ensure that words and phrases are separated by commas, with a space between each one. Here's an example:

> ice cream sundae, highly detailed, delicious, octane render, glistening, marshmallows, cherries

The order of the words and phrases isn't too important, but it's recommended to start with the main item (in this case, "ice cream sundae"). By following these guidelines, you're sure to generate excellent AI art images.

Utilize Advanced Prompts for AI Art Variations

If your AI-generated art isn't quite what you were hoping for, don't scrap it just yet. Instead, try using Midjourney's variation feature to achieve your desired outcome. To take full advantage of this tool, consider using advanced prompts to specify the changes you want to make. Here are some example prompts to consider:

- Style: Indicate a specific style, like "cyberpunk style," "grunge style," or "Pixar movie style," to tailor the art to your liking.
- Lighting and rendering: Use prompts like "softbox lighting," "cinematic lighting," or "octane render" to adjust the art's lighting and rendering.
- Chaos: Increase the level of abstraction using a number with the "chaos" prompt. For example, "Eiffel tower - -chaos 50" would produce a higher level of abstraction than "Eiffel tower - -chaos 10."

- Resolution: Specify the resolution you want with prompts like "4k," "8k," "ultra detailed," or "photorealistic." The "hd" and "quality" settings are also standard options, such as in the example, "/imagine beautiful young woman - -quality 7."
- Aspect ratio: Use prompts to specify the desired aspect ratio, such as "/imagine beautiful young woman - -quality 7 - -ar 4:3."
- Image prompts: Provide the URL of an existing image to make your AI art similar to it. For instance, "/imagine https://www.imgur.com/xyz1234 beautiful young woman - -quality 7."

Stay tuned for the next chapter, where we'll go over important considerations for selling AI-generated art.

CHAPTER 7

Things you Need to Consider before Selling AI Art

Computer programs implemented with AI techniques are now being utilized by artists to create original artwork in a specific visual style. Some view AI-generated work as a threat to human artists, as the software can produce similar pieces at a faster pace and more consistently than any human could ever manage.

On the other hand, some artists view the rise of AI-generated art as an opportunity for additional monetization or even as a stepping stone for their artistic careers. If you're considering selling your AI-generated art, there are several important factors to consider first.

Who is Your Target Audience and What is Your Goal?
The first aspect to consider is your target audience and why they might be interested in buying your work. Two main types of AI artists exist: generative and autonomous. Generative artists use an iterative process to create art, resulting in unique art pieces. Autonomous AI artists, on the other hand, use software to generate artwork in a specific visual style.

In other words, autonomous AI artists use advanced software to create artwork that fits a certain style. If your AI art is autonomous, you'll likely attract collectors and enthusiasts who want to own a piece of history.

When your AI art is generative, you could attract art buyers who want to own a unique, one-of-a-kind piece of artwork.

Determining the Value of Your AI Artwork

Once you've created your AI artwork, the next step is to determine its worth. The value of your work will depend on several factors. Consider the level of creativity in your work – highly creative pieces tend to fetch higher prices than generic ones.

The uniqueness of your work is the second factor. If your AI art is one-of-a-kind, you can charge more than if your works are commonplace. Note that in the United States, all AI art is considered unique, so you should have no problem describing your AI art as such when selling in this market.

In addition, the demand for your work will affect its price. High demand means you can charge more than if there's low demand. Finally, the availability of your work comes into play. If there are only a few original pieces of your work, you can charge more than if your work is readily available.

Understanding Your Target Audience and Optimal Sales Channels

Selling your art can be a challenging process, but knowing your audience and where to sell can make all the difference. If you're an autonomous artist looking to showcase and sell your work, art galleries are a great place to start. However, it's important to do your research before making any decisions.

Begin by researching galleries in your area to understand the types of artists they typically represent, and whether or not they accept autonomous AI art.

To boost your chances of success, create a show-worthy portfolio that includes images of your art, information about your background, and a price list. If possible, make an in-person visit to the gallery to personally hand off your portfolio.

Alternatively, you can send your portfolio by email if visiting each gallery isn't feasible. For generative AI art that you want to sell as a collector's item, online sales are the best option. Consider listing your work on popular websites like eBay or Etsy, or even starting your own website to promote your art.

Understanding Your Motivation for Selling AI Art

Your motivation for selling AI art can impact the price you receive for your work. If you're selling as an artist, you may demand a higher price than if you're selling as a business venture.

If you're selling as a collector who desires to own a piece of history, you'll likely be able to demand a higher price due to the artwork's value. Lastly, if you're selling as a business owner to fund future AI art projects, you may be able to command an even higher price due to the artwork's value.

Commercial Use: What You Need to Know

If you're interested in using AI art platforms like Midjourney, NightCafe, or DALL-E 2 for commercial purposes, you're in luck! Most of these platforms allow for commercial use, but there are some important considerations to keep in mind. For instance, with Midjourney, you'll need to be a paid member to sell your AI art. Meanwhile, NightCafe permits users to sell their creations, provided that they didn't knowingly use any copyrighted images while making the art. Keep in mind that rules for commercialization will vary from one AI art platform to another, so be sure to familiarize yourself with them before trying to sell your work.

CHAPTER 8

How to Sell your AI Art Online

Thanks to accessible online marketplaces such as Etsy, selling AI art has become a straightforward process. While there are only a few AI art vendors currently selling their products online, you can join their ranks. If you're interested in becoming an AI art vendor, we've compiled some advice to help you do so effectively.

Establish Your Following Prior to Selling

Prior to selling your AI art online, it would be ideal to cultivate a strong following. This is crucial for building a fan base, gaining exposure and testing the waters. If you have an active blog, Instagram account, or any other platform to showcase your AI art, you're already halfway there. Take advantage of this and establish yourself as an authority in your niche.

Picking the Perfect Online Marketplace for Your AI Art

There are many e-commerce platforms to choose from when selling your AI art. However, not all marketplaces are created equally, and some may be better suited for AI art sales than others. Etsy is a popular platform for selling handmade crafts and is a good choice for AI art sales.

Since AI art is a newer niche, you may have better success on a smaller platform like Shopify or Artsy. Take the time to explore various marketplaces before making a decision, but keep in mind that you may need to create separate accounts for each one.

This is especially true for selling your work online. Opening an Etsy shop is necessary if you intend to sell your AI art there. You might have to create a new account if you already sell handmade products on the platform.

Building an AI Art Portfolio
Creating a portfolio of your AI artwork is essential to establishing your online presence and showcasing your work to potential clients. By displaying your art over time, you can demonstrate how far you've come and entice customers to purchase your products.

There are many ways to host your portfolio, including social media accounts and personal websites. For a simple and straightforward approach, consider using a blog to collect and feature your artwork. Make sure to add links to your products on relevant marketplaces.

If you want to create a more professional looking portfolio website, it can be done inexpensively. Purchasing web hosting and a domain name that costs only a few dollars per month, as well as using free website builders like WordPress, are excellent options.

Crafting Persuasive Product Descriptions
Product descriptions are a vital aspect of selling your creations on any marketplace. These brief summaries are essentially sales pitches designed to showcase the unique qualities of your work and persuade customers to buy it.

It is important to note that not all potential customers may be familiar with the concept of AI art. Consequently, you should explain the concept using language that is suitable for all audiences. While you don't want to overwhelm the reader with technical terms, you also don't want to make the concept appear too outlandish. Otherwise, you risk losing potential customers.

Acquiring customers and making sales

After establishing your reputation and attracting a loyal audience, it's time to think about selling your work. You can find clients through social media marketing, paid advertisements, and online influencers.

Attending local events is also an option to meet potential customers in person and make sales. Keep in mind that online sales require perseverance since it's a lengthy and challenging process. Treat your online gallery like a legitimate business and stay committed to your goals.

CHAPTER 9

AI Art
Best Practices

For the best chance of success in creating in-demand AI art that sells, follow these eight essential practices:

AI Art: What It Is and How It Works

To succeed with AI art, it's vital to understand this innovative art form. By utilizing mathematical algorithms, AI art platforms can produce artwork automatically based on text instructions. No artistic ability or engineering expertise is necessary to create AI art, and it's becoming a popular medium for artistic expression.

AI art provides a unique look and can create pieces of high value. Once you become familiar with the features and prompts of your chosen AI art platform, it's easy to create AI art. Additionally, platforms are regularly introducing new features as the technology continues to evolve.

Exploring the Advantages of Crafting AI Art

Creating AI art has several benefits that can keep you motivated and inspired. The most significant advantage is that you don't need any artistic skills or experience to develop stunning AI art.

AI art platforms can help you choose colors, recognize facial features, and even handle repetitive tasks. That way, you can create art instantly without breaking a sweat. Plus, some platforms offer a marketplace for selling your AI creations.

Create Marketable AI Art

Many individuals who attempt to sell AI art often struggle to find buyers. Preparation is key in this field. To increase your chances of success, start by determining your target audience and identifying the types of AI art they are interested in. Experiment with various designs and layouts to determine the style that works best for you, and choose a platform that suits your needs.

It's important to have a solid understanding of how AI art is created and to master the right text prompts to use when generating your work. Finally, be sure to select a visual style that aligns with your artistic vision.

Selecting the Right Platform

To ensure that your requirements are met, it's essential to choose the right AI art platform. Here are six of the most popular AI art platforms to assist you: Midjourney, Jasper Art, Stable Diffusion (which is free), NightCafe, Photosonic, and DALL-E 2. All of these platforms, except for Jasper Art, offer a free trial so that you can try them out before making a decision.

Begin Your Journey with Midjourney

Midjourney is one of the leading AI art platforms available, and now you can sign up as a beta user without waiting. To utilize Midjourney, access to Discord is required. Start in the beginner's room to learn and test out the system. By using text prompts, you can easily create art, upscale your images, and generate variations.

Maximizing Your AI Art Results with the Best Text Prompts

Want to create stunning AI art? The key is in the text prompts that you use. To get started, familiarize yourself with the proper format for the text prompts on your AI art platform.

Use multiple adjectives and detailed descriptions to make your prompts more effective. Incorporate well-known words and specify the desired style. Looking for ideas? Explore a list of the most commonly used prompts, or get creative with advanced prompts for truly unique variations.

Key Considerations before Selling AI Art

Before diving into selling your AI art, there are several important factors to keep in mind. Who is your target audience and what is your motivation for selling? How much should your AI art be priced? Are you familiar with your audience's preferences and the most suitable venues to sell your AI art? Finally, is the AI art you have created available for commercial use?

Build a Following

Selling your AI art online can be a lucrative venture. Platforms like Etsy offer an excellent opportunity to showcase your work. However, before you get started, it's essential to build a following. Ensure that you select the right online marketplace for your art and build an impressive portfolio. Make sure to provide compelling descriptions that will draw in potential buyers.

CONCLUSION

By reading this guide in its entirety, you'll gain a strong understanding of how to produce AI art that caters to the market's demands and will fetch you the best price. It's crucial to avoid jumping in without proper knowledge.

Now it's time to put all the information into practice. While reading this guide is beneficial, you'll only achieve success by taking action and creating stunning AI art that's in high demand and can be sold for a premium price.

We hope this guide has been informative and valuable to you. Start by learning the basics of AI art and how it operates. We wish you all the best in creating AI art that's highly sought-after and profitable.

www.ingramcontent.com/pod-product-compliance
Lightning Source LLC
LaVergne TN
LVHW072050060326
832903LV00053B/316